The Common Core Readiness Guide to Reading™

TIPS & TRICKS FOR
SUMMARIZING
TEXT

Sandra K. Athans and Robin W. Parente

ROSEN
PUBLISHING®

New York

Published in 2015 by The Rosen Publishing Group, Inc.
29 East 21st Street, New York, NY 10010

Library of Congress Cataloging-in-Publication Data

Athans, Sandra K., 1958–
Tips & tricks for summarizing text/Sandra K. Athans and Robin W. Parente.—First Edition.
pages cm.—(The Common Core Readiness Guide to Reading)
Includes bibliographical references and index.
Audience: Ages 5–8.
ISBN 978-1-4777-7583-7 (library bound)—ISBN 978-1-4777-7585-1 (pbk.)—ISBN 978-1-4777-7586-8 (6-pack)
1. Rhetoric--Study and teaching—Abstracts. 2. Authorship—Abstracts. 3. Language arts (Elementary) I. Parente, Robin W. II. Title. III. Title: Tips and tricks for achieving mastery in summarizing text.
PE1477A74 2014
372.6′044—dc23
2013048463

Manufactured in the United States of America

Contents

Introduction

The Common Core Reading Standards are a set of skills designed to prepare you for entering college or beginning your career. They're grouped into broad College and Career Ready Anchor Standards, and they help you use reasoning and evidence in ways that will serve you well now and in the future.

The skills build from kindergarten to the twelfth grade. Grades six through eight take the spotlight here. You may have already noticed changes in your classrooms that are based on the standards: deeper-level reading, shorter passages, an emphasis on informational texts, or an overall increase in rigor within your daily activities.

This book will help you understand, practice, and independently apply the skills through easy-to-use "tips and tricks." Gaining mastery of the skills is the goal.

Your teachers may use *close reading* for some of their instruction. During close reading, you read shorter passages more deeply and analytically.

Close-reading passages often have rich, complex content. They contain grade-level vocabulary words, sentence structures, and literary techniques. Reading a short three-page passage closely could take a total of two to three days or more. The benefit to you is that you get a

The Common Core standards help build skills that are important for college or career readiness.

deeper, more valuable understanding of what you've read. Close reading is a critical part of the new Common Core Reading Standards and is used throughout this book.

Other well-known reading comprehension skills remain valuable. Visualizing, asking questions, synthesizing, and other traditional strategies work well together with the Common Core skills covered here.

This book focuses on the Anchor Standard 2: determining central ideas or themes of a text, analyzing their development, and summarizing key supporting details and ideas. In the next chapter, we'll break these skills apart and look at them closely. Also, the tips and tricks than can help you gain mastery of this standard are introduced. Some feature visual icons that will be used throughout this book.

In the passages that follow, you'll tag along with Expert Readers as they think aloud while closely reading from different passages of literature (fiction) and informational text (nonfiction). Ways in which the Expert Reader applies the tips and tricks appears in "Expert Reader" margin notes. You'll also *observe* the Expert Readers identify critical ideas and themes in passages, prepare written summaries, and respond to multiple-choice questions.

After you gain an understanding of how a skill is applied, it's your turn to try with guided practice. You'll apply the skill independently and perform a self-evaluation by checking your responses against the answers provided. Based on your responses, you can determine if another pass through the Expert Readers' examples might be helpful—or if you've mastered the skill.

CHAPTER 1

A QUICK AND EASY OVERVIEW: THE SKILLS AND THE TIPS & TRICKS

Let's examine the skills involved with determining central ideas or themes and constructing summaries closely so that we understand them. In order to prepare a strong summary, you need to first determine the central idea or theme of a text.

A central idea or theme is the overriding concept, a sort of *big picture* of meaning an author shares in his or her work. The central idea in an informational passage is the point the author stresses. It is comprised of the multiple details featured in the passage. In literature, the theme presents this big panorama of meaning. Although rooted in the characters and events of a particular story, a theme extends beyond the scope of the text and imparts a broader universal life lesson or idea. There may be more than one central idea or themes within a passage.

A summary is a brief statement of the central idea or theme of a text, together with the details that best support it. A summary is written in your own words, yet it should be objective. This means it should be free of personal opinions and judgments that cannot be supported through text evidence.

Determining a central idea or theme is an active reading skill and requires you to figure out the most important concepts in a text. You'll need to analyze, or carefully examine, how the author uses details to develop and convey the central ideas or themes to readers. You must also self-monitor your thinking as you read. This involves frequent, purposeful pausing to gauge the importance of information and ideas. Once you have identified the central ideas or themes, you are ready to construct a written or oral summary.

These skills are useful as you read literature and informational text, and in reading within history/social studies, science, and technical subjects. They're also useful for many of your real-life activities.

As you progress in grade levels, you're expected to consider more deeply how the themes or central ideas are developed in a text. For example, analyzing how the setting, plot, or other literary elements might contribute to the theme of a passage demonstrates the direction this skill development takes.

Tips & Tricks
Determining central ideas or themes and analyzing their development:

There are several easy-to-use tips and tricks that can help you determine the central idea or theme of a reading passage. Some are useful as you begin to read, while others guide you throughout your reading. Here's a quick overview of them. The icons featured below are used in subsequent chapters to show you how the tips and tricks are used in action with literature and informational texts.

 ● **Launching "Jump-Start" Clues** – Before you dive into reading a piece of text, skim and scan it quickly. Notice and take a visual inventory of everything you see, keeping in mind that you are gleaning the text for big ideas or its central meaning. The title can sometimes provide clues to the deeper-level central idea or theme. Callouts (text that is featured in a dramatic way, such as enlarged and boxed in a sidebar note) stress important dialogue, narration, or information. Visuals such as photographs, charts, graphs, and tables may feature events that support central ideas. Authors select and use text features purposefully. It's often helpful to ask yourself, "What could the title mean, or what meaningful ideas has the author stressed in the special features?"

G ● **Using the Genre of a Passage to Find Central Ideas and Themes and to Monitor Development** – Identifying the genre of a passage can often help direct your thinking about central ideas and themes. As you've learned, some literary genres serve specific purposes or contain elements that may suggest deeper-level concepts. For example, *pourquoi* stories (a form of folktale) were used to explain unknown events. Informational genres also serve specific purposes. For example, a speech presents someone's opinion on a matter and may contain language to persuade an audience. The purpose a genre serves may help you decipher its central idea and theme.

● **Using Text Structure (Flexibly) to Find Central Ideas and Themes and to Monitor Development** – Central ideas and themes may emerge early on and then develop throughout the passage. Determining what a passage is *mostly* about will help guide you to identify central ideas and themes, which may or may not be stated explicitly in the text. Gauge the volume of coverage or "weight" given to ideas, topics, or events. This usually equates to the value an author places on specific content.

You already know a lot about the different text structures. For example, in works of fiction, characters and a setting are introduced, a problem is identified, and events lead to a solution or improvement. With these works, it's helpful to consider how the character changes from the beginning to the end of the story. Ask yourself, "What lesson does the character learn?" Noting this change or others can help you refine your ideas about theme?

With informational text, authors organize ideas in sequential, cause-and-effect, or other structures that help readers grasp and remember important information. Identifying these structures can help guide and validate your ideas about central ideas. You might ask yourself, "Has the author linked ideas together using a cause-and-effect structure?" Also, authors of informational texts carefully organize information into paragraphs. Sometimes central ideas are expressed in topic or con-cluding sentences. Reviewing the paragraph structure can also help you spot central ideas.

 ● **Be Attentive to the Author** – It's important to detect what the author is saying in works of literature and in informational texts. In literature, the author often presents a life lesson or worthwhile idea that you take away from the story. Ask yourself, "What big idea is the author sharing with me?" Nonfiction and informational text is filtered through the author's perspective. Knowing this is important as you determine critical ideas he or she is presenting. It's helpful to ask yourself, "What point or issues has the author stressed?"

It's also important to recognize that the author may not explicitly tell you the life lesson or the major point or issue. Instead you have to infer this from clues. Some clues might be shrouded in a symbol. For example, birds might stand for freedom, or snakes might mean there is danger. Within a passage, reoccurring symbols can represent an idea or motif that contributes to the theme.

● **Recognize Topics of Common Themes** – The theme or critical idea of a passage may extend beyond the passage. It could represent universal values, emotions, or understandings. The degree to which a theme strikes a chord with readers can determine its appeal. Best sellers appeal to many people, and classic books or speeches endure the test of time because their themes continue to resonate with readers.

Within this context, it's easy to understand that common themes and critical ideas often emerge among works of literature as well as within informational passages. No doubt, you have uncovered many themes within your classes, some of which probably included the following topics:

- *Overcoming challenges*
- *Man against nature*
- *Accepting others' differences*
- *Friendship*

While reading informational texts, you also probably came upon passages that contained these common topics:

- *Leadership*
- *Awareness of the world*
- *Defending rights, correcting injustice, and fair treatment*
- *Stewards of the environment*

It could be helpful to keep these common or universal themes and ideas in mind as you read.

● **Tune In to Your Inside Voice** – Your mind is actively making sense as you read. Listening to your thoughts or your mind's *dialogue* helps you follow the development of central ideas and themes. Also tracking your feelings and views often helps you detect significant episodes and ideas that are likely to contribute to these deeper-level concepts. Monitoring your ongoing reaction to your reading is critical in helping you distinguish important ideas and themes.

Quick Check Self-Evaluation for Determining Central Ideas and Themes

Determining how well you've mastered the tips and tricks for determining central ideas and themes is important. One way to do this is by gauging your success with the following tasks:

✓ I have detected pivotal events and ideas that are stressed in the passage.

✓ I have identified recurring events and ideas that help shape larger, central ideas.

✓ The events and ideas I've chosen from the text interact cohesively in support of my view on a central idea and theme.

✓ The central idea or theme I've uncovered is fully supported by text evidence.

 ● **Avoid Common pitfalls** – Sometimes we can become distracted by something in the text, which could steer us away from an author's intended meaning. Staying engaged and focused while ensuring that your ideas square with evidence is critical. It's sometimes helpful to validate your interpretation by considering your response to the following statement: "I know this because…" Monitor your view of the critical idea or theme, and remain open to new interpretation. Over the course of the text, evidence may no longer support your original thinking, and it will be necessary for you to reconstruct or reshape your ideas. Don't mistake details for the central idea or theme, which is a larger concept.

As you practice and gain skill with these tips and tricks, you'll find that they work together and often become indistinguishable. This is a sure sign that they've become authentic and automatic, and kick in when and where they're needed.

Tips & Tricks

<u>Summarizing:</u> There are also some easy-to-use tips and tricks to help you prepare a summary of the text. Below you'll find a quick overview of them. Your success preparing a thoughtful and concise summary is practically guaranteed providing you set the stage by applying the tips and tricks for the first skills covered in this book.

- **A summary should include the central idea or theme *and* sufficient details from the text to support it.**
  It's critical to include these elements in a well-prepared summary. The absence of either will weaken or produce gaps in your presentation. Determining how much detail is sufficient could be a decision you're able to make on your own, or it may depend on length, time, or other guidelines or constraints you are given. How to tackle these constraints is described below.

If there are no constraints, your summary for a work of fiction could include brief descriptions of the character, problem, and solution, together with distinctive episodes or highlights from the beginning, middle, and end of a passage. In informational passages, you might wish to keep a running mental record of the gist of each paragraph until you build a noteworthy idea that is suitable to include in your summary. Subheading and other text features can help with this approach.

In sum, check on any guidelines or constraints you are expected to follow in preparing your summary, and then plan your approach accordingly.

Quick Check Self-Evaluation for Summarizing

Determining how well you've mastered the tips and tricks for summarizing is important. One way to do this is by gauging your success with the following tasks:

√ I have provided a succinct statement of the central idea or theme.

√ I have described how the central idea or theme is shown through specific details and examples from the text. My ideas are mostly expressed in my own words.

√ My summary accounts for events and ideas that occur over the course of the text.

√ My summary aligns with what the author likely intends and is distinct from my personal opinions and judgments.

- **Express the central idea or theme as a statement**

The manner in which you express the central idea or theme you've identified matters. Construct your idea as a statement. For example, it's not enough to say that the central idea of a passage is *about sources of alternative energy* or that the theme of the story is *about friendship*. Describing what is said or the author's contention about that topic is needed. For example, the main idea of the passage might be: locating alternative energy sources has gained momentum as a prime concern among our nation's leaders. Or the theme in the story could be: loyal friendships can be forged between people who may previously have been mortal enemies. Central ideas and themes are generally universal, valuable concepts and are worthy to be featured within a carefully constructed statement.

- **Sizing-up the quantity, quality, and order of your evidence**

Not all evidence is the same. Even though you may have already extracted important ideas from the text (from the skills you learned earlier in this book), you may still need to refine your pool of evidence.

14

Determining what to include and what to leave out can be tricky, especially in a short summary or in one you are writing under time constraints. The best details are those that support your ideas. Also consider the order in which you present your evidence, and lead with the strongest. Returning to the text to carefully consider these matters and gauging the strength of evidence is helpful.

- **Building evidence for inferential thinking**

When information, events, a character's motive, or other ideas are implied but not explicitly stated, you base your thoughts, feelings, and views on clues. Returning to the passage and locating these clues is how you *build a case* for your ideas. Making sure your ideas align or square with text clues ensures that you're interpreting the passage in a way the author likely intended. Exercise care when you use inferential evidence as support in your summary.

- **Paraphrase details in your own words**

When preparing your summary, it's OK to use character dialogue, excerpted text, or key phrases as they appear in the text (along with proper citation). However, information used in this manner should be justified, and it should support an original idea. Much of your summary will rely on paraphrased events intermingled with strong, original ideas.

- **Avoid common pitfalls**

Misinterpreting any part of the text can occur when your thinking doesn't square with text evidence. Always ask yourself if your thinking is most likely what the author intended. Make sure your summary is objective, distinct from your personal opinion and judgment. Review your summary to ensure that the support details you've chosen are vital, not simply interesting. Also remember that a summary is not a retelling—you are only featuring *important* ideas, not *all* ideas.

CHAPTER 2

DETERMINING CENTRAL IDEAS OR THEMES AND SUMMARIZING LITERATURE: EXPERT READER MODEL

Let's see how to apply the tips and trick to literature. Remember that literature could be adventure stories, historical fiction, mysteries, myths, science fiction, realistic fiction, allegories, parodies, and more.

Literature often features elements such as characters, problems or conflicts, a setting and plot, events and episodes, and a problem resolution. Awareness of the structure helps a reader follow the story and improves comprehension of the passage.

Specific genres within literature also have specific characteristics and features. For example, science fiction contains elements of the supernatural, and dramatic plays contain scripted character dialogue. As mentioned earlier, some works of fiction may even serve a purpose (such as pourquoi stories) that can help you with your analysis. Your ability to identify central ideas or themes and construct a summary relies on your grade-level knowledge of these literature basics.

Grade-level knowledge of literature basics provides a solid foundation to support the Common Core Reading Standards.

Plan of Action

The passage in this chapter is an excerpt from *Myths of the World: The Ancient Chinese*. You'll be reading the passage and following an Expert Reader think through a sampling of the tips and tricks in the margin notes. It's as if you're tagging along with the Expert Reader.

You'll also *observe* the Expert Reader prepare a T-chart in which information has been extracted from the text to uncover and build a case for a theme. Next, you'll see how the Expert Reader uses this information to construct a cohesive summary. Finally, you'll tag along while the Expert Reader works through several multiple-choice questions that explore other ways in which text evidence is used to determine the theme of the passage.

🏃 An Excerpt from *Myths of the World: The Ancient Chinese*

by Virginia Schomp

📖 EXPERT READER:

🏃 Based on the title and subtitle, this appears to be a passage specific to the Chinese culture. It refers to "ancient" times and may therefore be folklore or historic. The distinction that it covers the creation of the sky and earth suggests it is a creation story.

G The first two paragraphs confirm 🪜 my thinking about the genre – this passage is a creation story because it seeks to explain how a world came to be from a formless, swirling mass of desolation. Although I'm not familiar with "Pangu," his role as creator and child of the universe implies his importance.

G Based on my knowledge of this genre, I now expect to learn how natural objects in the world came to be.

Pangu Creates the Sky and the Earth

Long ago, at the beginning of time, heaven and earth were mingled together. All was the same, in a vast empty universe. All was dim and misty, formless and endless, a swirling desolation.

It is said that this mass of confusion was shaped like a giant chicken's egg. At the heart of the egg, Pangu was born. Pangu was the first of all beings, the child of the forces of the universe. **G**

For countless ages Pangu slept inside the egg. Finally, he woke up and stretched his arms. The shell of the egg cracked, and everything inside poured out. The light and pure parts that were yang floated up and became the sky. The dark and heavy parts that were yin sank down and became the earth. **G**

Pangu was pleased with the separation of the sky and earth, but he feared that they would not remain divided. So he stood with the blue sky resting on his head and his feet pressing down on the yellow earth. The sky rose higher, the earth sank deeper, and Pangu grew taller in the space between them. G

For eighteen thousand years, Pangu stood like a pillar. Each day the sky rose ten feet higher, and the earth sank ten feet deeper. Each day Pangu grew ten feet taller, until he had grown into an enormous giant.

At last the sky reached its highest height, and the earth reached its lowest depth. Pangu saw that the two were fixed firmly in place. Never again would the world dissolve into chaos. G

Signing with relief, the giant lay down to rest from his long labors. He breathed deeply one last time and drifted into a peaceful death. As he died, his breath was transformed into the wind and clouds. His voice became the rolling thunder. His left eye rose as the sun, his right eye as the moon. The hairs of his head and beard turned into the countless stars. The sweat of his brow streamed down as the life-giving rain.

EXPERT READER:

G — The problem in this story is emerging – Pangu fears the earth and sky will blend together and revert back to a mass of formless desolation. I'll monitor this to determine if it develops.

— Pangu's reaction – to stand like a pillar for eighteen thousand years – shows his dedication and selfless sacrifice. These ideas are not from "an author" per se, but could be important as cultural values. I'm going to monitor the development of these ideas.

G — Maybe the problem is solved and will not recur. I'll have to monitor this.

— Pangu is relieved to prevent the return of chaos, yet interestingly he is unable to witness further creation. Let's see the direction this idea might take.

— I know that "sacrifice" is a common topic for themes in literature. After learning that Pangu drifted into a peaceful death after creating a world, I'm considering that the story could support a theme having to do with sacrifice. It seems connected with my earlier ideas on the value of dedication and selfless sacrifice.

The other parts of the giant's body became the features of the earth. His trunk and limbs turned into the sacred mountains of the five directions: north, south, east, west, and center. His flesh formed the fertile fields. His muscles and veins became the paths that humans would travel. The hairs on his body grew as the grass, plants, and trees. His blood flowed into the seas, lakes, and rivers. His teeth and bones became rock and metal, while the marrow of his bones hardened into precious pearls and jade. The dying body of Pangu even gave rise to living beings, when the tiny specks on his skin sprang forth as the fish and animals.

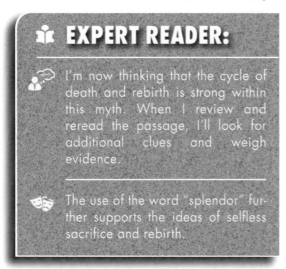

EXPERT READER:

I'm now thinking that the cycle of death and rebirth is strong within this myth. When I review and reread the passage, I'll look for additional clues and weigh evidence.

The use of the word "splendor" further supports the ideas of selfless sacrifice and rebirth.

And so it was that the firstborn, Pangu the giant, brought order out of chaos and filled heaven and earth with all their splendors.

Quick Check Self-Evaluation for Determining Central Ideas and Themes

Let's pause here to let the Expert Reader gather and sift through some of the pivotal events and ideas that were featured in the story and to identify recurring ideas that were presented. As the Expert Reader collects this information, the central theme(s) will emerge.

Pivotal Events and Ideas	• In the beginning of time, heaven and earth were mingled together into a mass of confusion.
	• Pangu, child of the forces of the universe, was born into this egg-shaped mass.

Pivotal Events and Ideas	• He one day awoke, stretched, and cracked open the egg shell, releasing the light part to the sky (yin) and the heavy parts (yang) to the earth. • For eighteen thousand years Pangu stood like a pillar, securing the separation of sky and earth, which he feared would revert into chaos. During that time, he had grown into a giant. • Once the earth and sky were secure, Pangu died peacefully and his body became components of the earth.
Recurring Ideas	• Chaos is a fearful and undesirable state of being. • Seeking and maintaining order over chaos is viewed as a monumental or "giant" achievement.
Central Theme(s)	• The world and its splendor were nurtured into existence. • Perseverance can result in great accomplishment. • New life arises from death.

Now that the Expert Reader has detected some central theme(s) as well as details to support them, preparing a thoughtful summary should be trouble-free. The Expert Reader will select key details to use as evidence, paraphrase ideas, and avoid unsupported opinions or judgments.

According to an ancient Chinese myth, Pangu awoke from within an egg-like mass of chaos and created order.

Expert Reader's Summary

Pangu Creates the Sky and the Earth is an ancient Chinese creation myth that suggests the world in all its splendor was nurtured into existence through perseverance, fortitude, and selfless sacrifice. According to the myth, the firstborn child of the forces of the universe, Pangu, awoke from within an egg-like mass of chaos. He was pleased as the sky and the earth that spilled during his awakening took shape and moved into position to launch order within the universe. Still, he feared that the two emerging regions might easily blend together and revert into disorder. To prevent this, he wedged himself between them like a pillar, and remained there for eighteen thousand years. During that time, Pangu grew taller as the space between the sky and earth became greater. Once the sky and earth had reached fixed places and were safe from chaos, the giant-sized Pangu signed with relief and died peacefully. His body became the features of the earth.

    Expert Reader: I'm pleased with this summary. I feel confident that the theme I selected squares with text evidence, and I have presented critical ideas in my summary. Now I'm ready to challenge my thinking by answering multiple-choice questions.

    (Notice that in some cases, more than one answer may be considered correct. It's important to build a case for the best answer by carefully reviewing the passage and gauging the evidence.)

Mini Assessment

1. Which detail *best* supports the central theme that the world was nurtured into existence?

    a) For eighteen thousand years, Pangu stood like a pillar.
    b) The sweat of his brow streamed down as life-giving rain.
    c) His voice became the rolling thunder.
    d) For countless ages Pangu slept inside the egg.

2. Establishing order over chaos was a tremendous undertaking. What symbolism in the story *best* supports this claim?

a) Pangu slept inside the egg for countless days, and his voice became the rolling thunder.

b) Pangu slept inside the egg for countless days, and he had grown into an enormous giant.

c) Pangu stood like a pillar, and his voice became the rolling thunder.

d) Confusion was shaped like a giant chicken's egg, and Pengu had grown into an enormous giant.

3. Which event *best* represents a turning point in the story?

a) The light and pure parts that were yang floated up and became the sky.

b) The dark and heavy parts that were yin sank down and became the earth.

c) At last the sky reached its highest height, and earth reached its lowest depth.

d) It is said that this mass of confusion was shaped like a giant chicken's egg.

Check your answers. Were you correct?

1. a) is the best answer. To nurture means to safeguard and develop. By separating the sky and earth for eighteen thousand years, Pangu was protecting the safe development of the world. Although Pangu gave of himself in choices b and c, these actions would not have been possible without the events in choice a happening first.

2. d) is the best answer. Although many of the choices contain references to giant-like—or tremendous—events or activities, those in d are most pertinent to harnessing chaos. In the other choices, I either question the "symbolism" and/or was unable to link both examples to overcoming chaos.

3. c) is the best answer. After the earth and sky finally arrived at their fixed safety points, Pangu transformed into the features and creatures of the earth. Although choices a and b could be turning points, they are not featured together in a single answer.

Expert Reader: I'm satisfied with my responses. In all cases, I returned to the text to check against evidence. Sometimes the evidence was right there, explicit in a character's actions or words. Other times I had to dig a little deeper and use clues and inferences and carefully weigh my thinking. In either case, I can argue in support of my answers with credible evidence from the text.

Conclusion

How well have you grasped the Expert Reader's use of the tips and tricks to determine central ideas or themes and construct summaries? Decide if you're ready to move on to the guided practice in the next chapter or if you would like to take another pass through the Expert Reader's model.

CHAPTER 3

DETERMINING CENTRAL IDEAS OR THEMES AND SUMMARIZING LITERATURE: GUIDED PRACTICE

Now it's time for you to apply the tips and tricks during your close reading of a passage. The practice prompt icons will guide you. Check to see if your responses to the prompts match the provided possible responses.

🖥 GUIDED PRACTICE PROMPT:

🏃 What jump-start clues do you notice? (Possible response: From the title and subtitle, I suspect this passage may be a creation myth from the Maya culture.)

An Excerpt from 🏃 *Myths of the World: The Ancient Maya*
by Virginia Schomp

The Great Flood 🏃

Here is how it was before time began. There was not earth. There was not one rock, tree, or meadow. Not one bird, fish, animal, or person.

There was only the sea, all alone in the darkness. In the sea lay a god, rippling and murmuring. The god was clothed in glittering blue-green feathers that gave him his name: Gucumatz, the Plumed Serpent.

And of course there was the sky above the sea. The blank sky stretched out endlessly over the vast expanse of the waters. In the sky was the god Huracan, whose name means Heart of Sky.

Huracan looked out over the blackness and longed for the dawn. G He went down to the sea and spoke to the Plumed Serpent. The gods talked and they thought. In their great wisdom, they dreamed up a vision of how the world should be. They saw the earth set apart in the midst of the waters. They saw the growth of trees and

Preparing a concise, well-constructed summary often involves collecting and organizing evidence-based ideas in a graphic organizer such as a T-chart.

🖥 GUIDED PRACTICE PROMPT:

G What do you notice about the genre and its structure? (Possible response: I can confirm that this passage is a creation myth. It begins with a bleak picture of what things were like before the earth was created. Two important gods have also been introduced.)

How is the text structure helping you here? (Possible response: In this type of myth, I can expect that the earth will be created along with man. I also know that values of this culture will be reflected in this important myth. These values could be themes.)

27

GUIDED PRACTICE PROMPT:

What important ideas have been passed down in the retelling of this creation myth? (Possible response: The gods envisioned that the people they created would honor and respect them through praise, prayer, and sacrifice. This was an expectation. I'll monitor this idea to see how it develops.)

Does the topic "fit" as a common theme in this genre? (Possible response: The idea that people should show humbleness to their creator makes sense in a creation myth.)

GUIDED PRACTICE PROMPT:

What are you thinking? (Possible response: The idea that animals should also praise the gods supports my idea that worship is important. The animal's response also suggests a brewing problem.

bushes. They saw a race of people who would praise them and nurture them with prayers and sacrifices.

Then the gods said, "Earth." And from their word the earth was formed. It arose suddenly, like a cloud billowing up from the waters. Great mountains soared into the sky, dividing the sea into lakes and rivers. The face of the earth sprouted a blanket of cypress and pine trees.

The gods were pleased with their creation. "It is good that you came to me," the Plumed Serpent said to Heart of Sky. "Our design has turned out well. Now let us fill the world with living creatures."

So the gods thought of all the animals. From their thoughts and words, the deer and birds emerged. The gods gave the deer a home in the meadows, canyons, and forests. They established nests for the birds in the trees and bushes. They also brought forth jaguars, pumas, serpents, and all the other creatures.

"Now speak out," the gods commanded. "Praise those who have made you." But the animals just squawked and howled and chattered.

"This has not turned out well," said Heart of Sky and the Plumed Serpent. "They cannot name our names and praise us." So the gods told the animals that they would have to serve in another way. They must offer their flesh to be eaten. All the animals, small and great, would become food for the praise giver who had not yet been created.

A second time the gods tried to make a creature who would nurture them with prayers and sacrifices. This time they worked with the earth. They mixed the earth with water and formed the mud into the shape of a man. But the creature did not look right. Its face was lopsided, and it could not stand or walk. It could talk, but its words were just sounds without meaning.

"This has not turned out well," said the gods. "Creatures made from mud cannot live and multiply." So Heart of Sky and the Plumed Serpent broke up the image they had created.

Twice the gods had tried and failed to make a praise giver. Before trying a third time, they asked for the help of Grandfather Xpiyacoc and Grandmother Xmucane. These ancient diviners are older than all the other gods. They know how to read the secrets of the universe, and at last came their answer: "Let there be a race of wooden people."

GUIDED PRACTICE PROMPT:

What are you thinking? (Possible response: It seems the gods will try another praise-giver, a creation that is likely to be man.)

It's surprising to me that the people created of the earth—typically a prized entity in a creation myth—lacked looks and sense.

What important ideas have been passed down in the retelling of this creation myth? (Possible response: I have a lot of evidence to support the theme that devotion to the creators is essential. Another emerging theme may be that man must have the "sense" to recognize the value of their creation through honoring the creators. I'll monitor these ideas.)

How is the text structure helping you here? (Possible response: I think that the materials the people are created from may be meaningful. Perhaps another theme is emerging. I'll monitor this, too.)

What are you thinking? (Possible response: Wood seems to be the material of choice for man? Wood seems to be an inferior choice than material from the earth. I'm beginning to doubt my initial ideas about the importance of the materials the gods used to create man.)

"So be it," replied the creators. The moment they spoke, it was done. The earth was populated with people made from wood. At first, the people seemed to be a success. They looked and talked like humans. But the wooden people had no blood or sweat. Their skin cracked, and their arms and legs warped in the heart. Worst of all, their minds and hearts were empty, so they had no memory of their creators. They just wandered around aimlessly, doing whatever they wanted. They mistreated their animals and neglected their household utensils, making the millstones screech and burning the cooking pots. They did not call upon their makers in the prayer or nurture the gods with sacrifices.

Heart of Sky and the Plumed Serpent were disappointed and angry. The people made from wood were not worthy to live on the face of the earth. So the gods sent a catastrophe to destroy them. The sky turned black. The rains began to fall. In the midst of the storm came four ferocious demons. When the people fled into their houses, everything they had abused turned against them.

And so the people made from wood were crushed and drowned

and scattered. Only a few survived the wrath of the creators. Today, their descendents still scamper through the forests, a reminder of the wooden people who forgot their creators.

**GUIDED PRAC-
TICE PROMPT:**

What are you thinking? (Possible response: I'm surprised the myth has ended without the creation of man. I would suspect that there is another myth that continues this beginning.

Quick Check Self-Evaluation for Determining Central Ideas and Themes

Remember: Now that you've read through the passage and identified some important details and targeted some ideas as larger concepts or themes, it's time to reread the passage. In your rereading, sift through and build evidence for your ideas. Are the ideas stressed? Do they recur to shape a larger idea?

Let's try it. Talk through your ideas or record and organize them into a graphic organizer like a T-chart or another type you've used in class. Use the guided practice prompts if you are uncertain.

Pivotal Events and Ideas	• At one time, there was no earth, only sea and darkness. • The gods, Huracan (Heart of Sky) and Gucumatz (the Plumed Serpent), envisioned a world and commanded it into existence. • Next, they created animals. But as the creatures were unable to give praise to the gods, they became the food for those who could. • The gods tried to make new creatures out of the earth, but the mud people

Pivotal Events and Ideas	were also a disappointment. They looked odd, and their words were meaningless. • The wiser ancient gods (Xpiyacoc and Xmucane) were asked to help. They advised that a new race be created of wood. • The wood people were also a disappointment. Their hearts were empty, they often neglected things around them, and they even forgot their creators. Deemed unworthy, they were destroyed.
Recurring Ideas	• Man's humility and devotion to the gods is critical. • Good sense, judgment, and heart are highly respected.
Central Theme(s)	• Man's worthiness and permanence in the world is dependent upon on his ability to worship and praise the gods honorably. • Those who pass on neglect and mistreatment will likely encounter similar misfortune.

Now that you've identified a major theme (or themes) and have pulled the details from the text that support your ideas, it's time to construct a summary. Use the information you've collected. Remember to clearly state and then support the theme using mostly your own words. The evidence you select must support your ideas. Try to talk through your summary or write it down on a separate piece of paper. (See Expert Reader's summary.)

According to the ancient Maya creation myth, the creation of the world was complex and marked by trial and error. This was largely because of the troublesome task of creating suitable creatures to occupy it.

Expert Reader's Summary

In the ancient Maya creation myth of the Great Flood, a theme that emerges suggests that man's worthiness and permanence in the world are reliant upon his ability to worship and praise the gods honorably. According to the myth, the creation of the world was complex and marked by trial and error. While the earth was easily envisioned and commanded into existence, the creation of the creatures that would occupy it was troublesome. The creator gods, Huracan and Gucumatz, were displeased with all three of their attempts, which included animals, a people made from mud, and a people made from wood. In all cases, the gods were disappointed that their creations were unable to worship and praise them honorably. All lacked some degree of heart, good sense, and/or physical appeal—and thus lacked a devoted ability to worship through heart, body, and mind. All were unworthy.

Once you're satisfied with your summary and have checked your response with the one provided by the Expert Reader, you might want to challenge your thinking and tackle some multiple-choice questions.

(Remember to use evidence to square your thinking and selection of the *best* answer. Return to the passage while considering the theme and the important support details you identified.)

Mini Assessment

1. Which of the following sentences from the passage *best* helps the reader begin to define a central theme of the text?

    a) Huracan looked out over the blackness and longed for the dawn.

    b) In their great wisdom, they dreamed up a vision of how the world should be.

    c) They saw a race of people who would praise them and nurture them with prayers and sacrifices.

    d) "Now let us fill the world with living creatures."

2. Which of the sentences from the story *best* demonstrate a key idea that people should treat others in the manner in which they wish to be treated?

    a) "Worst of all, their minds and hearts were empty, so they had no memory of their creators."

    b) "Each and everything that the people had abused turned against them."

c) "But the animals just squawked and howled and chattered.

d) "Only a few survived the wrath of the creators."

3. Which statement *best* describes how the theme developed over the course of the story?

a) The animals were unable to express their devotion, the creatures made of wood looked and sounded human-like but they were spiritless, and the creatures made of mud could only make meaningless sounds and were lifeless.

b) The animals were a useful source of food, the mud creatures looked and acted human-like but they could not talk, and the creatures made of wood did not look human-like and they lacked spirit.

c) The animals were unable to express their devotion, the creatures made of mud sounded human-like but they were spiritless, and the creatures made of wood could only make meaningless sounds and were lifeless.

d) The animals were unable to express their devotion, the creatures made of mud could only make meaningless sounds and were lifeless, and the creatures made of wood looked and sounded human-like but were spiritless.

Check your answers. Were you correct?

1. c) is the correct answer. The central idea of the story is that man's worthiness and permanence in the world are based on his ability to worship and praise the gods honorably. Selection c, which appears early on in the story, *best* introduces this idea.

2. b) is the correct answer. The creatures made of wood "mistreated their animals and neglected their household" and in the end, "everything that the people had abused turned against them." The cause-and-effect relationship between these two ideas establishes the key idea that people should treat others in the manner in which they wish to be treated.

3. d) is the correct answer. This answer correctly presents the sequence of the three creatures and correctly describes the shortcomings of each. The other responses are either incorrect sequences or do not correctly pair the shortcoming to the creature.

Conclusion

How well have you grasped the tips and tricks to determine central ideas or themes in literature and construct summaries? Based on your performance and self-evaluation, decide if you're ready to move on to the next chapter or if you would like to take another pass through this guided practice.

CHAPTER 4

DETERMINING CENTRAL IDEAS OR THEMES AND SUMMARIZING INFORMATIONAL TEXT: EXPERT READER MODEL

Now let's see how to apply the tips and tricks to informational text. Remember, informational text is a type of nonfiction, or factual text, that is written to inform the reader, explain something, or convey information about the natural and social worlds. Informational text can include newspaper and magazine articles, essays, speeches, opinion pieces, editorials, and historical, scientific, technical, or economic accounts.

Authors of informational text have a point to make about a topic. They frequently want to change your thinking in some way or add to your understanding. These authors purposefully organize their ideas by using a problem/solution, descriptive, compare/contrast, chronological/sequence, or cause/effect text structure. Awareness of these structures helps a reader determine central ideas and improves comprehension.

Plan of Action

Similar to chapter 2, you'll be reading a passage while following an Expert Reader think through the tips and tricks—this time as they are applied to informational text. You may want to refresh your memory by reviewing the tips and tricks before beginning.

Again, you'll *observe* the Expert Reader perform a self-evaluation through the sharing of a T-chart where information is gathered and sifted to uncover the central idea of the text, followed by the construction of a cohesive summary. Finally, you'll tag along while the Expert Reader works through several multiple-choice questions that explore the full impact of using text evidence to determine central ideas when constructing summaries.

Then, in the chapter that follows, it will be your turn to practice. You'll start by reading a passage where guided practice prompts and icons cue your use of the tips and tricks. You can check your thinking against provided possible responses.

🏃 An Excerpt from
Perspectives On: The Titanic Tragedy
by Jeff Burlingame

📖 EXPERT READER:

🏃 Noticing the title, headings, and subheadings will help me begin to glean the central idea of this passage. Awareness of the specific words selected for these text features may provide insight into author's perspective.

An "Unsinkable" Ship
The Gilded Age

The wreck of the *Titanic* occurred during America's Gilded Age, a period lasting from roughly the mid-1860s until the early 1900s, that saw the rise of powerful corporations and

"The starlight night was beautiful"

Stern
2nd class
Section of ship

"The Titanic looked enormous"

Boat Deck
clear of boats

"Every porthole
& saloon was
blazing with light"

"We had sixty
or seventy
on board"

The bows & bridge
completely under water

Loose floating
ice

"Sea-calm as a pond
There was just a gentle heave"

Many have questioned if safety and the lives of innocent people were sacrificed in order to provide an opulent travel experience for wealthy travelers aboard the *Titanic*.

that was defined by its extravagance and exploitation. The privileged class of the Gilded Age flaunted its wealth in many ways. Travel was one of them, and the *Titanic* had been created with this clientele in mind. Its purpose was to dominate the North Atlantic luxury travel market by offering an opulent experience the likes of which had never been seen. Were safety and the lives of 1,500 innocent people sacrificed to achieve this goal?

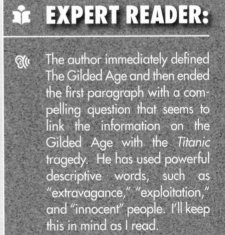

📖 EXPERT READER:

The author immediately defined The Gilded Age and then ended the first paragraph with a compelling question that seems to link the information on the Gilded Age with the *Titanic* tragedy. He has used powerful descriptive words, such as "extravagance," "exploitation," and "innocent" people. I'll keep this in mind as I read.

The lessons learned from this disaster continue to impact the way the shipping industry is regulated. With each large-scale maritime tragedy since, new rules have been created. Even some one hundred years after the *Titanic*'s sinking, the importance of learning from history's best-known maritime disaster has not diminished. 🎭

EXPERT READER:

This paragraph is interesting. It talks of learning lessons from disasters and tragedies. I'll tuck this away as I continue reading.

Battle for Sea Supremacy

To gain market share, shipping lines focused not only on building the biggest, most luxurious ships but also on making them capable of crossing the ocean as quickly as possible. In the early 1900s, John Pierpont "J.P." Morgan, one of the most powerful and richest men in the world, bought the White Star Line, and the company formulated a plan to create three superliners that would be among the most luxurious and largest vessels the world had ever seen. The thought of Gilded Age travelers basking in luxury left the owners of the White Star Line dreaming of the profits they could make, should superior numbers of travelers choose their ship over others'. ✍

EXPERT READER:

I connect this paragraph to the introductory paragraph. The phrase "dreaming of the profits they could make" makes me uneasy when I think of the earlier question concerning the safety and lives of innocents.

In March 1909, work on the *Titanic* began. Thanks to Morgan's financial backing, cost was not a great issue in building the *Titanic*, and more than three thousand men worked for three straight years to build it. The total cost to build the *Titanic* was $7.5 million, or roughly $400 million in today's currency. The measures used to keep costs down would become important issues of debate following its sinking.

A Catastrophic Collision

On April 10, 1912, *Titanic* left on its maiden voyage. The evening of April 14, 1912, pointed to another quiet night at sea for *Titanic*'s passengers and crew, until 11:40 PM when the lookouts spotted a massive iceberg directly in the ship's path. The first officer was quick to act and a head-on collision was avoided, but as the ship passed to the left of the iceberg, the starboard side of the hull scraped the iceberg. When the situation was assessed, it was found that the ship's hull had been punctured and water was flooding six of the sixteen compartments, which had been designed to make *Titanic* "unsinkable."

>
> ### EXPERT READER:
>
> After reading the final sentence of this paragraph, again I am uneasy and am wondering what the measures to keep costs down were. Did this contribute to the *Titanic* tragedy?

> ### EXPERT READER:
>
> There is no question this is informational text. The author is presenting facts, and I am learning some interesting information I may not have been aware of. I'll remember that authors use informational text to persuade a reader to think or feel a certain way.

Not Enough Lifeboats for All

Stewards rushed from room to room, waking passengers and directing them to the boat deck, where other crew members helped them put on life belts, but the loading of the lifeboats was chaotic. Lifeboats that left before the severity of the situation had been fully recognized were not full, but even if all the lifeboats had been filled to capacity, nearly five hundred people would have been stranded on the sinking vessel, since the ship's twenty lifeboats could carry only 1,178 people and there were 2,224 passengers and crew on board.

Early designs of the ship featured enough boat lifts to hold an adequate number of lifeboats, but those lifts would have taken up much of the room on the first, and second, class promenade decks, an area passengers used to walk around the entire outside of the ship. Much of *Titanic*'s lavishness would have been lost if more lifeboats were added. Also, carrying a sufficient number of lifeboats would have added to the ship's cost and thus eaten away at the owners' profits.

> **EXPERT READER:**
>
> I recognize the cause/effect text structure. I can identify several events leading up to the tragedy and why these events happened. Could this tragedy have been avoided?

The issue of too few lifeboats was not exclusive to the *Titanic* or to the White Star Line. It was rare for any of the larger ships of the day to carry enough lifeboats to accommodate everyone. The British Board of Trade required only sixteen lifeboats for a ship over 10,000 tons. The *Titanic* weighed 46,000 tons and exceeded these criteria and therefore, was not in violation. However, these rules were very outdated and they had not been amended since 1894, when the largest ship on the seas was about 13,000 tons. The *Titanic* was several times heavier and, consequently, able to carry far more people.

> **EXPERT READER:**
>
> I'm thinking back to the earlier mention of learning from disasters. Wasn't it just common sense to have enough lifeboats to hold all the people on board? Did they really need a law to tell them that? I remember the owners of the White Star Line dreaming of profits. Did greed outweigh common sense and safety?
>
> Could more people have been saved if different decisions had been made during *Titanic*'s construction? Do rules and regulations exist to protect people? Could this be the central idea of this passage?

In the end, only 706 people were lucky enough to get spots in the *Titanic*'s lifeboats, eventually to be pulled aboard the *Carpathia* and taken safely to New York. Killed were 1,518 passengers and crew.

Quick Check Self-Evaluation for Determining Central Ideas and Themes

Let's take a break here to let the Expert Reader gather and sift through some of the pivotal events and ideas stressed in the passage and identify the recurring events and ideas. As the Expert Reader collects this information, the central idea will begin to emerge. Remember, authors of informational text want to change your thinking in some way or add to your understanding, so the Expert Reader will think about the most important ideas being discussed in each section of the text. She'll make certain that the events and ideas chosen interact cohesively. As a result, the central idea that is eventually uncovered will be fully supported by text evidence.

Pivotal Events and Ideas	• The Gilded Age was a period when the wealthy expected great luxury when they traveled. • The *Titanic* was built in response. • The owners of the Titanic expected to make a great deal of money from travelers, especially if costs could be kept down. • Original ship design allowed for an adequate number of lifeboats, but owners decided to include fewer. • Fewer lifeboats meant more space on the first - and second - class promenade decks for passengers' recreational use. • Fewer lifeboats kept costs down. • Safety rules at the time required only

Pivotal Events and Ideas	a minimum of sixteen lifeboats on board. • After the collision, there were not enough lifeboats to carry all passengers. • The ship sank; 1,518 people died while only 706 people were rescued.
Recurring Ideas	• Extravagance/lavishness • Profits and cost-cutting measures • Number of lifeboats • Safety rules and regulationsv
Central Theme(s)	• Profits (money) should not be more important than the safety of people. • Rules should exist to protect innocent people.

Now that the Expert Reader has determined a central idea and has collected details from the text to support it, constructing a thoughtful and concise summary is simple. She'll choose the details that best support the central idea, paraphrase it in her own words, and align the summary with what the author most likely intended, which is distinct from her own personal opinions and judgments.

Expert Reader's Summary

As a result of the sinking of the *Titanic* and the deaths of 1,518 people on board, rules and regulations were put into place to protect people traveling on ships. The *Titanic* tragedy occurred during the Gilded Age, which was a time when the wealthy expected great luxury when they traveled. The *Titanic* was built to be lavish and extravagant. In order to provide more luxury, the number of lifeboats was reduced. The owners were aware that there were not the proper amount of lifeboats on board, but they chose to ignore that fact. The rules and regulations of the time did not require the owners to place additional lifeboats on the ship. As a result, when the *Titanic* sank, not everyone on board was able to fit into the lifeboats, and 1,518 people died. Following this tragedy, rules and regulations were updated to help ensure the safety of all people traveling by ship.

Expert Reader: I'm satisfied with this summary. I've thought about the passage carefully, I've reread some sections to check my understanding against text evidence, and I've used key ideas to support the central idea. I'm ready to challenge my thinking by answering multiple-choice questions.

Notice that in some cases, more than one answer may be considered correct. It is important to use evidence to build a case for the *best* answer. Carefully reviewing evidence by returning to the passage will be helpful, and gauging which response is best supported through the evidence is critical.

Mini Assessment

1. Which of the following sentences from the text *do not* help to build the central idea that rules are frequently put in place to protect people?

    a) The thought of Gilded Age travelers basking in luxury left the owners of the White Star Line dreaming of the profits they could make.

    b) The measures used to keep costs down would become important issues of debate following its sinking.

    c) The lessons learned from this disaster continue to impact the way the shipping industry is regulated.

d) Much of the *Titanic*'s lavishness would have been lost if more life-boats were added.

2. One central idea of the text is that profits sometimes take precedence over safety. Which sentence from the text develops this idea?

a) Lifeboats that left before the severity of the situation had been fully recognized were not full.

b) Early designs of the ship featured enough boatlifts to hold an adequate number of lifeboats, but those lifts would have taken up much of the room on the first- and second-class promenade decks, an area passengers used to walk around the entire outside of the ship.

c) Thanks to Morgan's financial backing, cost was not a great issue in building the *Titanic* and more than three thousand men worked for three straight years to build it.

d) Even some one hundred years after the *Titanic*'s sinking, the importance of learning from history's best-known maritime disaster has not diminished.

3. Which central idea does the author communicate by including details about the Gilded Age?

a) The Gilded Age was an important time period in history.

b) Safety should be an important consideration when dealing with large numbers of people.

c) The promise of profits can sometimes cloud good judgment.

d) Rules and regulations are frequently put into place to protect people.

Check your answers. Were you correct?

1. a) is the best answer, as it only speaks to the profits the owners anticipated and does not help build the central idea concerning rules and safety. Answers b), c), and d) build the central idea that rules are frequently put into place to protect people.

2. b) is the best answer. The owners made a conscious decision to trade safety for profits when they changed the number of lifeboats on board Titanic.

3. c) is the best answer. The ship was designed to carry all passengers in lifeboats, but was changed to meet what the owners thought wealthy customers wanted in a luxury ship. Their judgment was clouded when they made the decision to trade safety for profits.

Expert Reader: I'm satisfied with my responses. In all cases, I returned to the text to check against evidence. At times, I had to dig deeply into the text and use clues and inferences while carefully weighing my thinking. I'm confident I can argue in support of my answers with credible evidence from the text.

Conclusion

How well have you grasped the Expert Reader's use of the tips and tricks to determine central ideas or themes and constructing summaries? Decide if you're ready to move on to the guided practice in the next chapter or if you would like to take another pass through the Expert Reader's model.

CHAPTER 5

DETERMINING CENTRAL IDEAS OR THEMES AND SUMMARIZING INFORMATIONAL TEXT: GUIDED PRACTICE

Now it's time for you to apply the tips and tricks during your close reading of a passage. The practice prompt icons will guide you. Check to see if your responses to the prompts match the provided possible responses.

GUIDED PRACTICE PROMPT:

 What jump-start clues do you notice? (Possible response: The title and headings give me a clue as to what the central idea may be. Looking at the headings and the clue word "journalism" in the title will help me define "muckrakers."

An Excerpt from *The Muckrakers: American Journalism During the Age of Reform*
by Aileen Gallagher

Exposing the Truth

The United States grew at such a rapid pace during the Industrial Revolution that the country experienced growing pains. A sharp rise in population, corrupt business and political practices, and social injustice led to a turn-of-the-century reform movement known as the Progressive Era (*c.* 1900–1920). Some of the greatest contributors of this era of reform were investigative journalists known as muckrakers.

In 1890, many people across America read a book called *How the Other Half Lives* by Jacob Riis. It told the story of the poor who packed the tenement slums of New York City. Americans did not know anything about these tenements, which were small, dark, and often windowless apartments. The tenements were originally built for single families, but New York's growing population needed places to live. Soon, tenement apartments were divided into smaller units that housed many families. Americans did not know that these crowded apartments often made people sick.

Things began to change after people learned about the slums. New tenement buildings were bigger. They had more light and fresh air. Children could play in playgrounds instead of in the streets. *How the Other Half Lives* made people recognize inadequate conditions and work to reform them.

After *How the Other Half Lives* was published, other writers began to expose society's ills, too. They wrote about children who went to work instead of go to school. They wrote about companies that broke laws, and they wrote about rotten things in food that made people sick. These writers were called muckrakers because they "dug" up the

GUIDED PRACTICE PROMPT:

How can you use text structure to find the central idea? (Possible response: Noticing how the author has linked ideas together, as well as how much coverage or weight she gives to certain ideas, helps me sift through information. The descriptive text structure explains the Progressive Era. I notice words like "corrupt," "social injustice," and "reform.")

GUIDED PRACTICE PROMPT:

Be attentive to the author. (Possible response: I'm noticing the recurring idea of "Americans did not know." This might be helpful later when determining the central idea(s).)

How is the text structure helping you? (Possible response: The author purposefully changed from a descriptive structure to a cause/effect structure. What does she want me to focus on?)

truth, or muck. People read articles and books by the muckrakers and wanted things to change. Often, people in power also learned about situations that needed improvement by reading the muckrakers' articles.

Going Undercover

In 1888, journalist Elizabeth Cochrane, who went by the name of Nellie Bly, decided to write about a textile factory. She didn't just visit the factory, however. Instead Bly got the story by working there. She wanted to know what working in a factory was really like. Today, reporters call this style of investigation "going undercover." In the factory, Bly met girls who should have been in school. Instead they worked to help support their families. The girls had to squint to see what they were doing because the light in the factories was so poor. Few of them could afford to buy glasses. In some cases, the girls' eyesight worsened because of such conditions. G

Next, Bly went undercover at a mental hospital to learn what living conditions were like for the mentally ill. To get her story, she pretended to be insane in September 1887, and city workers believed her. She was sent to the Women's Lunatic Asylum on Blackwell's Island. Inside the asylum were women who were physically ill, illiterate, and poor. Although few of them were insane, the hospital would not release them.

Bly spent ten days on Blackwell's Island before representatives from the *New York World* newspaper could get her released. Her stories were published and the people in New York began to pay attention to Blackwell's asylum. Hundreds wrote letters to the newspaper demanding something be done to help the women. The city took notice, too. Bly's articles sparked a city investigation of activities on Blackwell's Island. A muckraker had changed things again.

GUIDED PRACTICE PROMPT:

What are you thinking? (Possible response: Nellie Bly's reporting on her undercover findings must have been sensational at the time. These paragraphs remind me of the power that ordinary people can have when they want something changed.)

Change

Sometimes the truths muckrakers exposed did not immediately change laws. More often than not, the muckrakers' stories changed people's minds and made readers want to learn about other problems in their country. The nation was ready for change, and the muckrakers examined everything. Later, they wrote about greedy corporations, race relations, child labor, the pharmaceutical industry, and how food goes from the farm to the dinner table.

GUIDED PRACTICE PROMPT:

Are you starting to recognize an important central idea common in informational text? (Possible response: In this text we have the muckraker who exposes problems and the ordinary people who demand change once they become aware of wrongdoings. What central idea statement might work?)

What are you thinking? (Possible response: After reading, I'm able to sort and sift ideas to develop a central idea that is supported by significant details.)

Muckrakers helped make America safer and better for its people. Although the Progressive movement has ended, journalists still rake the muck. Contemporary muckrakers still write about children, the poor, disease, and greedy business practices. As long as the world has problems, muckrakers will continue to write about and expose them to effect positive reforms.

Quick Check Self-Evaluation for Determining Central Ideas and Themes

Remember: At this point, it's important that you pause and reread with the purpose of gathering and sifting through the pivotal events and ideas in the passage to identify the recurring events or ideas. As you do this, the central idea will become clearer, and you'll have the text evidence to support it. Once you have that, constructing the summary will be simple.

Let's try it! (Refer to page 12 for quick check self-evaluation criteria.) Talk through your ideas or jot them down using a graphic organizer, like the T-chart below. Use the guided practice prompts to guide you if you are uncertain. (See page 54 for an Expert Reader's take on this section.)

Pivotal Events and Ideas	
	• The Progressive Era was a reform movement that addressed corruption and social injustices.
	• Once problems are uncovered, people want them resolved.
	• Investigative journalists called muckrakers wrote books and articles exposing the corruption and injustices.
	• Many problems were uncovered.
	• Once Americans read the books and articles, they demanded change.
	• America became safer and more just as a result.

Recurring Ideas	• Corruption and social injustices sometimes occur because people are unaware. • Once uncovered, people want problems resolved. • Change comes from knowledge.
Central Theme(s)	• Knowledge is powerful and can cause change that improves the safety and lives of people.

Now that you've determined a central idea and have collected the details from the text to support that idea, it's your turn to construct a thoughtful and concise summary. Use the information gathered in the T-chart to clearly state your central idea and support it with text evidence. Remember to paraphrase and keep your personal opinions and judgments separate. Keep in mind what the author most likely intended for you to learn from the article. Try your summary now by talking it through or jotting it down on a separate piece of paper. (See page 54 for the Expert Reader's summary.)

Nellie Bly was a muckracker who went undercover to expose social injustices.

Summary: Investigative reporting by journalists called muckrakers proved how powerful knowledge can be in making change occur. Corruption and social injustices were rampant in America in the early 1900s. Most Americans were unaware of these issues until muckrakers exposed them in books and articles. Once Americans learned of these problems, they demanded change to stop the corruption and injustices uncovered. As a result of the knowledge that Americans obtained because of the muckrakers' reporting, change occurred that made America a safer and more just place to live. Knowledge is powerful in making change happen.

(Your summary may be somewhat different from the Expert Reader's, and that's OK as long as it holds up under scrutiny and squares with the supporting text evidence you've chosen to use to support the central idea.)

Once you're satisfied with your summary and have checked your response with that of the Expert Reader above, it's time to challenge your thinking through the answering of some multiple-choice questions.

Again, be aware that it is important to use evidence to build a case for the *best* answer. Remember to carefully review evidence by returning to the passage and thinking about the central ideas that you've uncovered. Gauging which response is *best supported* through the evidence is critical.

Mini Assessment

1. Which of the following details from paragraph two of the excerpt *best* helps the reader begin to define a central idea of the text?

　　a) In 1890, many people across America read a book called *How the Other Half Lives.*
　　b) It told the story of the poor who packed the tenement slums of New York City.
　　c) Americans did not know anything about these tenements.
　　d) The tenements were originally built for single families.

2. Which of the following sentences from the article *best* helps to build the central idea that knowledge is powerful?

a) In the factory, Bly met girls who should have been in school.

b) The girls had to squint to see what they were doing because the light in the factory was so poor.

c) Bly went undercover at the mental hospital to learn what living conditions were like for the mentally ill.

d) Her stories were published, and the people of New York began to pay attention.

3. One central idea of the text is that muckrakers were important to the reform that occurred during the Progressive Era. Which sentence from the text *best* develops this idea?

a) More often than not, the muckrakers' stories changed people's minds and made readers want to learn about other problems in their country.

b) Sometimes the truths muckrakers exposed did not immediately change the laws.

c) Some of the greatest contributors of this era of reform were investigative journalists called muckrakers.

d) She (Bly) didn't just visit the factory, however. Instead Bly got the story by working there.

Check your answers. Were you correct?

1. c) is the best answer. This question assumes that you have already determined the central ideas of the text, one of which is when people learn of social injustices or corruption, they strive for change to make life more just for all. Americans did not know of the conditions in tenements, but once they found out, they demanded change. Thus, knowledge is powerful in effecting change, which is a central idea of this text.

2. d) is the best answer. Once people read Bly's stories, they became knowledgeable about social injustices and corruption that was occurring in their city and demanded change. This supports the central idea that knowledge is powerful.

3. a) is the best answer. The question refers to the reform that occurred during the Progressive Era. It's important to recognize that "reform" is another word for "change." Answer a) acknowledges that muckrakers changed people's minds and made them want to learn about problems. When they learned of problems, they demanded change or reform.

Conclusion

How well have you grasped the tips and tricks needed to determine central ideas or themes in informational text and construct summaries? Based on your performance and self-evaluation, decide if you've mastered the skills or if you would like to take another pass through this guided practice. Congratulations if you're ready to move on!

A New Expert Reader!

Now that you've mastered how to use the tips and tricks for determining central ideas or themes in informational text and constructing summaries, you're on your way to becoming an Expert Reader! Continue practicing with different types of literature and informational texts. You'll see that your attempts to grapple with classroom and assigned texts are far easier now.

GLOSSARY

ANALYZE To carefully examine, inspect, and consider a text in order to fully understand it.

CENTRAL IDEA The key concept or message being expressed.

CLOSE READING The deep, analytical reading of a brief passage of text in which the reader constructs meaning based on author intention and text evidence. The close reading of a text enables readers to gain insights that exceed a cursory reading.

DISTRACTOR Anything that steers a reader away from the text evidence and weakens or misguides analysis.

EVIDENCE Information from text that a reader uses to prove a position, conclusion, inference, or big idea.

FIX-UP STRATEGIES Common techniques used when meaning is lost.

GENRE A system used to classify types or kinds or writing.

INFERENCE A conclusion that a reader draws about something by using information that is available.

INFORMATIONAL TEXT A type of nonfiction text, such as an article, essay, opinion piece, memoir, or historical, scientific, technical, or economic account, that is written to give facts or inform about a topic.

LITERATURE Imaginary stories, such as mysteries, myths, creation stories, science fiction, allegories, and other genres that include elements such as characters, problems, conflicts, setting, plot with events or episodes, and problem resolution.

OBJECTIVE To be based on facts, rather than feelings or opinions.

PARAPHRASING Restating someone else's ideas while preserving the meaning of the original source.

POINT OF VIEW The perspective, or position, from which the story is told.

SUMMARY A short account of a text that gives the main points but not all the details.

TEXT FEATURES The variety of tools used to organize text and give readers more information about the text.

TEXT STRUCTURE The way in which information is organized within a written text.

Council of Chief State School Officers
One Massachusetts Avenue NW, Suite 700
Washington, DC 20001-1431
(202) 336-7000
Website: http://www.ccsso.org
The Common Core State Standards Initiative is a state-led effort coordinated
by the National Governors Association Center for Best Practices (NGA
Center) and the Council of Chief State School Officers (CCSSO). The
standards provide a clear and consistent framework to prepare students
for college and the workforce.

National Parent Teacher Association
12250 North Pitt Street
Alexandria, VA 22314
(703) 518-1200
Website: http://www.pta.org
National PTA enthusiastically supports the adoption and implementation by
all states of the Common Core State Standards. The standards form a
solid foundation for high-quality education.

New York State Education Department
89 Washington Avenue
Albany, NY 12234
(518) 474-3852
Website: http://www.engageny.org
EngageNY.org is developed and maintained by the New York State Education
Department. This is the official website for current materials and
resources related to the implementation of the New York State P–12
Common Core Learning Standards (CCLS).

Partnership for Assessment of Readiness for College and Careers

1400 16th Street NW, Suite 510

Washington, DC 20036

(202) 745-2311

Website: http://www.parcconline.org

The Partnership for Assessment of Readiness for College and Careers is a consortium of eighteen states plus the District of Columbia and the U.S. Virgin Islands working together to develop a common set of K–12 assessments in English and math anchored in what it takes to be ready for college and careers.

U.S. Department of Education

Department of Education Building

400 Maryland Avenue SW

Washington, DC 20202

(800) 872-5327

Website: http://www.edu.gov

Nearly every state now has adopted the Common Core State Standards. The federal government has supported this state-led effort by helping ensure that higher standards are being implemented for all students and that educators are being supported in transitioning to new standards.

Websites

Due to the changing nature of Internet links, Rosen Publishing has developed an online list of websites related to the subject of this book. This site is updated regularly. Please use this link to access the list:

http://www.rosenlinks.com/CCRGR/Summ

BIBLIOGRAPHY

Beers, Kylene, and Robert E. Probst. *Notice & Note: Strategies for Close Reading*, Heinemann: Portsmouth, NH, 2013

Burlingame, Jeff. *The Titanic Tragedy* (Perspectives On). New York, NY: Marshall Cavendish Benchmark, 2011.

Fountas, Irene C., and Gay Su Pinnell. *Genre Study: Teaching with Fiction and Nonfiction Books*. Heinemann, Portsmouth, NH, 2012

Gallagher, Aileen. *The Muckrakers: American Journalism During the Age of Reform*. New York, NY: Rosen Publishing, 2006.

Schomp, Virginia. *The Ancient Chinese* (Myths of the World). New York, NY: Marshall Cavendish Benchmark, 2009.

Schomp, Virginia. *The Ancient Maya* (Myths of the World). New York, NY: Marshall Cavendish Benchmark, 2009.

INDEX

About the Authors

Sandra K. Athans is a national board-certified practicing class-room teacher with fifteen years of experience teaching reading and writing at the elementary level. She is the author of several teacher-practitioner books on literacy, including *Quality Comprehension* and *Fun-tastic Activities for Differentiating Comprehension Instruction*, both published by the International Reading Association. Athans has presented her research at the International Reading Association, the National Council of Teachers of English conferences, and the New York State Reading Association conferences. Her contributions have appeared in well-known literacy works, including *The Literacy Leadership Handbook* and *Strategic Writing Mini-Lessons*. She is also a children's book writer and specializes in high-interest, photo-informational books published with Millbrook Press, a division of Lerner Publishing Group.

Athans earned a B.A. in English from the University of Michigan, an M.A. in elementary education from Manhattanville College, and an M.S. in Literacy (birth–grade 6) from Le Moyne College. She is also certified to teach secondary English. In addition to teaching in the classroom, she is an adjunct professor at Le Moyne College and provides instruction in graduate-level literacy classes. This spring she was awarded Outstanding Elementary Social Studies Educator by the Central New York Council for the Social Studies. Athans serves on various ELA leadership networks and collaborates with educators nationwide to address the challenges of the Common Core Standards. The Tips & Tricks Series is among several Common Core resources she has authored for Rosen Publishing.

Robin W. Parente is a practicing reading specialist and classroom teacher with over fifteen years of experience teaching reading and writing at the elementary level. She also serves as the elementary ELA coordinator for a medium-sized district in central New York, working with classroom teachers to implement best literacy practices in the classroom. Parente earned a B.S. in elementary education and an M.S. in education/literacy from the State University of New York, College at Oswego. She is a certified reading specialist (PK–12) and elementary classroom teacher and has served on various ELA leadership networks to collaborate with educators to address the challenges of the Common Core Standards. The Tips & Tricks series is among several Common Core resources she has authored for Rosen Publishing.

Photo Credits